D1090951

00001820087320

Dive into Division

Division

Lisa Arias

Rourke
Educational Media

rourkeeducationalmedia.com

Before Reading:

Building Academic Vocabulary and Background Knowledge

Before reading a book, it is important to tap into what your child or students already know about the topic. This will help them develop their vocabulary, increase their reading comprehension, and make connections across the curriculum.

1. *Look at the cover of the book. What will this book be about?*
2. *What do you already know about the topic?*
3. *Let's study the Table of Contents. What will you learn about in the book's chapters?*
4. *What would you like to learn about this topic? Do you think you might learn about it from this book? Why or why not?*
5. *Use a reading journal to write about your knowledge of this topic. Record what you already know about the topic and what you hope to learn about the topic.*
6. *Read the book.*
7. *In your reading journal, record what you learned about the topic and your response to the book.*
8. *After reading the book complete the activities below.*

Content Area Vocabulary
Read the list. What do these words mean?

array

compatible numbers

distributive property

dividend

divisor

equation

estimate

factors

inverse operations

power of ten

product

quotient

remainder

After Reading:

Comprehension and Extension Activity

After reading the book, work on the following questions with your child or students in order to check their level of reading comprehension and content mastery.

1. *How are the partial quotients strategy and long division strategy similar? How are they different? (Summarize)*
2. *Why does the remainder have to be smaller than the divisor? (Asking questions)*
3. *Which strategy of estimation do you use? Why? (Text to self connection)*
4. *How is multiplication used in division? (Summarize)*
5. *How can pictures help you when dividing? (Asking questions)*

Extension Activity

Everyday division! Go to the grocery store with your parents and notice the products they buy. Are there different quantities for some items? For example, everyone needs toilet paper, so locate that aisle and see what the better deal is between two brands. How many rolls do you get for the dollar amount? How would division help you get the cost per roll? Now check the price per roll for the other brand. Which is the better deal? Try looking at other products too. Not only will you become a master at division but you will be a smart shopper!

Table of Contents

what IS DiViSioN?

Soon you will decide your favorite way to divide.
No matter which method you choose, just be aware
you are splitting a number into equal groups, fair and square!

Dividing 12 by 3 is really just splitting 12 into 3 equal groups.

Signs for Division

Division problems can be written in many ways.
No matter what division sign you see,
their meanings simply agree.

$$12 \div 3$$

$$12/3$$

$$3\overline{)12}$$

$$\frac{12}{3}$$

Check It Out!

What a surprise.
Fractions are division
problems in disguise!

Each number of a division problem has a special name, some of which sound very strange!

$$12 \div 3 = 4$$

Dividend   Divisor   Quotient

When a number cannot be divided evenly, the amount left over is the **remainder**.

It is a rule and is always true that remainders must be smaller than the **divisor**.

$$19 \div 5 = 3 \quad R4$$

Dividend   Divisor   Quotient   Remainder

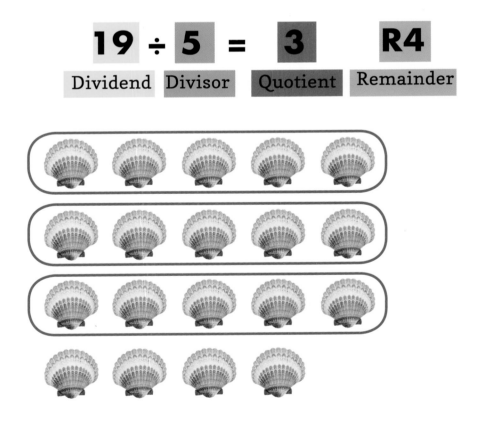

Relate Division to Multiplication

Multiplication and division are **inverse operations**.

Inverse operations work together to create fact families.

$$12 \div 3 = ?$$

With the help of fact families, you can solve any division problem by thinking of its matching multiplication fact.

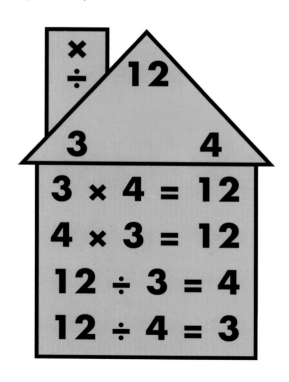

Use basic facts to find each **quotient** and matching multiplication fact.

$$32 \div 4$$

$$100 \div 10$$

$$42 \div 7$$

$$63 \div 9$$

Answers:

$32 \div 4 = 8$ because $8 \times 4 = 32$

$100 \div 10 = 10$ because $10 \times 10 = 100$

$42 \div 7 = 6$ because $6 \times 7 = 42$

$63 \div 9 = 7$ because $7 \times 9 = 63$

SOlVe EQuationS

What number divided by 3 equals 2?

$$w \div 3 = 2$$

Using inverse operations is what you do
to solve division equations for me and you.

$$w \div 3 = 2$$

Since 2 × 3 = 6, then 6 ÷ 3 = 2.

Check It Out!

A variable is a letter or symbol in place of an unknown number.
$z \div 9 = 3$ or $\frac{z}{9} = 3$

Use basic facts to find each quotient and matching multiplication fact.

$$n \div 5 = 15$$

$$\frac{s}{11} = 5$$

$$a \div 4 = 7$$

$$\frac{t}{6} = 3$$

Answers:

$75 \div 5 = 15$ because $15 \times 5 = 75$

$\frac{55}{11} = 5$ because $5 \times 11 = 55$

$28 \div 4 = 7$ because $7 \times 4 = 28$

$\frac{18}{6} = 3$ because $3 \times 6 = 18$

Models

Division arrays are models used to show each part of a division **equation**.

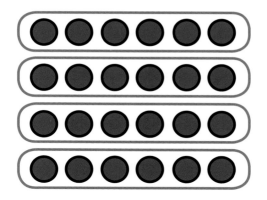

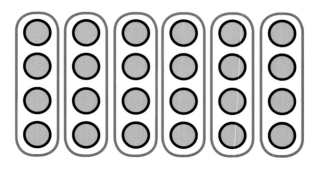

24 ÷ 4 = 6

Number in all (Dividend) Number of groups (Divisor) Number in each group (Quotient)

24 ÷ 6 = 4

Number in all (Dividend) Number of groups (Divisor) Number in each group (Quotient)

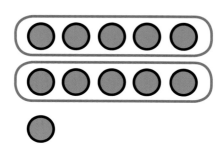

No need to fear if remainders appear!

11 ÷ 2 = 5   R1

Number in all (Dividend) Number of groups (Divisor) Number in each group (Quotient) Remainder

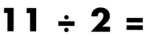

Name the division equation shown in each **array**.

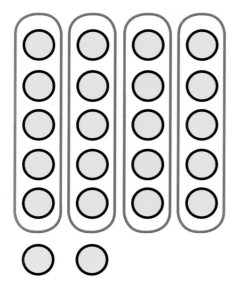

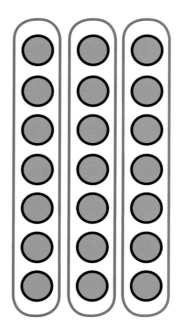

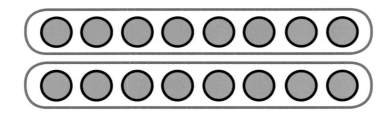

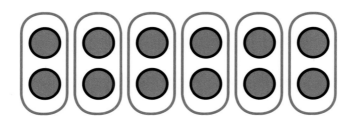

Answers:
22 ÷ 4 = 5R.2
21 ÷ 3 = 7
16 ÷ 2 = 8
12 ÷ 6 = 2

Powers of 10 Patterns

The patterns of powers of ten are key
to dividing numbers easily.

Let's see the pattern flow
when numbers begin to grow.

35 ÷ 7 = 5

350 ÷ 7 = 50

3,500 ÷ 7 = 500

35,000 ÷ 7 = 5,000

As you can see,
the zeros match up quite nicely.

When dividing a **power of ten** by another, cancel a zero in the
dividend for each zero in the divisor.

45 ÷ 5 = 9

45̶0̶ ÷ 5̶0̶ = 9

4,50̶0̶ ÷ 5̶0̶ = 90

45,00̶0̶ ÷ 5̶0̶ = 900

Cancelling zero pairs is really cool
because it shrinks numbers so nicely for you.

Use power of ten patterns to find each quotient mentally.

12,000 ÷ 4 =
12,000 ÷ 40 =
12,000 ÷ 400 =
12,000 ÷ 4,000 =

36 ÷ 6 =
360 ÷ 6 =
3,600 ÷ 6 =
36,000 ÷ 6 =

24,000 ÷ 8 =
24,000 ÷ 80 =
24,000 ÷ 800 =
24,000 ÷ 8,000 =

33 ÷ 3 =
330 ÷ 3 =
3,300 ÷ 3 =
33,000 ÷ 3 =

33,000 ÷ 3 = 11,000
3,300 ÷ 3 = 1,100
330 ÷ 3 = 110
33 ÷ 3 = 11

36,000 ÷ 6 = 6,000
3,600 ÷ 6 = 600
360 ÷ 6 = 60
36 ÷ 6 = 6

24,000 ÷ 8,000 = 3
24,000 ÷ 800 = 30
24,000 ÷ 80 = 300
24,000 ÷ 8 = 3,000

12,000 ÷ 4,000 = 3
12,000 ÷ 400 = 30
12,000 ÷ 40 = 300
12,000 ÷ 4 = 3,000

Answers:

Rectangle Method

Rectangle arrays break up large division problems on the spot when numbers grow too large to model with dots.

$$336 \div 3$$

Begin with a blank rectangle array that represents the total being divided. Label the side with the divisor.

$$3 \boxed{336}$$

Next, multiply by the divisor, using powers of ten and friendly multiplication. Keep track of the **factors** along the top and their totals inside until the amount being divided has been decided.

$$\times \ \ 100 + 10 + 2 = 112$$
$$3 \ \boxed{300 + 30 + 6} = 336$$
$$336 \div 3 = 112$$

Any chunk you choose is just fine.
Your model does not have to look exactly like mine!

Even with rectangle arrays,
remainders can still come out to play.

$$1{,}970 \div 9 = 218 \text{ R}8$$

$$\begin{array}{c} \times \quad 100 + 100 + 10 + 8 = 218 \\ 9\,\boxed{900 + 900 + 90 + 72} = 1{,}962 \end{array}$$

$$\begin{array}{r} 1{,}970 \\ -1{,}962 \\ \hline 8 \end{array}$$

Use friendly facts and powers of 10 to get as close as you can to the dividend. If the numbers are unable to divide fair and square, the amount left over is the remainder.

Estimation

Before you divide, use estimation to make a prediction.

Estimation helps you decide
if your answer should be disqualified.

Choose any strategy because estimation can be done
in more ways than one.

Compatible Numbers

Friendly numbers are a breeze to divide mentally. Either number will do. The divisor can run the show or just simply begin with the dividend.

You can see that 10 and 299 are not **compatible numbers** because 10 only evenly divides into numbers that end in zero. To **estimate**, round 299 to the closest number that ends with zero.

$$299 \div 10$$
$$300 \div 10 = 30$$
$$299 \div 10 \approx 30$$

Now you know, that your answer should be just below the number 30. The symbol ≈ means: is approximately equal to.

You can estimate high or you can go low. Just do your best to adjust to the closest compatible pair, fair and square.

243 ÷ 3
240 ÷ 3 = 80   Change the divisor to 240
243 ÷ 3 ≈ 80   because 3 × 8 = 24.

700 ÷ 8
720 ÷ 8 = 90   Change the dividend to 720
700 ÷ 8 ≈ 90   because 8 × 9 = 72.

Power of 10 Rounding

Once the numbers begin to grow,
adjust to the closest power of 10 you know.

449 ÷ 46   **785 ÷ 71**
450 ÷ 50 = 9   **800 ÷ 80 = 10**
449 ÷ 49 ≈ 9   **785 ÷ 71 ≈ 10**

892 ÷ 286
900 ÷ 300 = 3
892 ÷ 286 ≈ 3

Front-End Estimation

Front-end estimation is a really great tool
to find a quotient's range for me and you.

$$7\overline{)4{,}289} \quad \text{?xxx}$$

Because 7 cannot divide into a smaller
number, join the 4 with 2 to make 42.

$$7\overline{)4{,}289} \quad \text{6xx}$$

$7\overline{)42}$ is 6. So, the first digit is 6 and
it is in the hundredths place.

$$7\overline{)4{,}289} \quad \text{6xx}$$

Now you are done! Front end
estimation just showed you that the
quotient is between 600 and 700.

$$7\overline{)4{,}289} \quad \text{612 R5}$$

Yes the range is correct.
4,289 ÷ 7 is between 600 and 700.

Check It Out!

The range is a spread of numbers; one
low and one high.

Use front-end estimation to find the range of each quotient.

$$3\overline{)988}$$

$$8\overline{)6{,}574}$$

$$39\overline{)397}$$

$$52\overline{)6{,}053}$$

Answers:

3)988 is between 300 and 400 because 9 ÷ 3 = 3

8)6,574 is between 800 and 900 because 65 ÷ 8 ≈ 8

39)397 is between 10 and 11 because 39 ÷ 39 = 1

52)6,053 is between 100 and 200 because 60 ÷ 52 ≈ 1

Multiplication Check

Time to see how multiplication guarantees your answer's accuracy.

For Quotients without Remainders

Multiply the quotient by the divisor. The **product** should equal the dividend. If it does not, then you have just discovered an error.

$$3 \overline{)159} = 53$$

$$\begin{array}{r} 53 \\ \times 3 \\ \hline 159 \end{array}$$

For Quotients with Remainders

First multiply the quotient by the divisor. Next, add the remainder to the product. This answer should equal the dividend. If it does not, then you have discovered an error.

$$4 \overline{)371} = 92 \text{ R3}$$

$$\begin{array}{r} 92 \\ \times 4 \\ \hline 368 \end{array}$$

$$\begin{array}{r} 368 \\ +3 \\ \hline 371 \end{array}$$

Yes or No? Multiply to verify if each quotient is correct.

$$\begin{array}{r} 25 \text{ R3} \\ 5\overline{\smash{)}128} \end{array}$$

$$\begin{array}{r} 23 \\ 6\overline{\smash{)}139} \end{array}$$

$$\begin{array}{r} 42 \\ 6\overline{\smash{)}252} \end{array}$$

$$\begin{array}{r} 26 \text{ R4} \\ 7\overline{\smash{)}180} \end{array}$$

Answers:

Yes
$25 \times 5 = 125$
$125 + 3 = 128$
No
$23 \times 6 = 138$

Yes
$42 \times 6 = 252$
No
$26 \times 7 = 182$
$182 + 4 = 186$

Distributive Property Division

Splitting up dividends into friendly numbers is easy to do with the help of the **distributive property** for me and you.

Time to see how the distributive property can help to solve 69 ÷ 3.

First split 69 into numbers that are compatible with 3.

60 + 9

Next, find the quotient of each part.

60 ÷ 3 = 20

9 ÷ 3 = 3

Finally, add the quotients.

20 + 3 = 23

As you can see, dividing a number by its parts is the same as dividing the whole number from the start.

69 ÷ 3 = 23

Check It Out!

Check Your Quotient:

$$\begin{array}{r} 23 \\ \times\ 3 \\ \hline \checkmark\ \overline{69} \end{array}$$

Use the distributive property to divide 192 by 8.

First, split 192 into numbers that are compatible with 8.
Since 8 × 2 = 16, then 8 × 20 = 160.

160 + 32 = 192

Next, find the quotient of each part.

160 ÷ 8 = 20

32 ÷ 8 = 4

Finally, add the quotients.

20 + 4 = 24

Final Answer:

192 ÷ 8 = 24

Check Your Quotient:

$$\begin{array}{r} 24 \\ \times\ 8 \\ \hline \sqrt{192} \end{array}$$

Partial Quotients

Using partial quotients to divide, gives you control of how things go.

$$
\begin{array}{r}
118 \\
7 \overline{)826} \\
-700 \quad 100 \\
\overline{126} \\
-70 \quad 10 \\
\overline{56} \\
-56 \quad +8 \\
\overline{0 \mid 118}
\end{array}
$$

Begin by subracting powers of 10 away from the dividend.
7 × 100 = 700
7 × 10 = 70

Next, subract multiplication facts.
7 × 8 = 56

When all that's left is zero or the remainder, relax and add all of your facts.

Check It Out!

Check Your Quotient:

$$
\begin{array}{r}
118 \\
\times \ 7 \\
\hline
\checkmark\ 826
\end{array}
$$

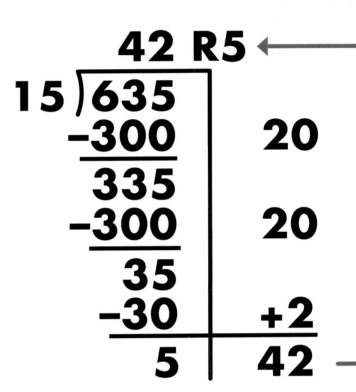

$$15 \overline{)635}$$ → **42 R5**

−300	20
335	
−300	20
35	
−30	+2
5	42

Begin by subracting powers of 10 away from the dividend.

$15 \times 20 = 300$

$15 \times 20 = 300$

Next, subtract multiplication facts.

$15 \times 2 = 30$

When all that's left is zero or the remainder, relax and add all of your facts.

Check It Out!

Check Your Quotient:

$$\begin{array}{r} 15 \\ \times 42 \\ \hline 630 \end{array} \qquad \begin{array}{r} 630 \\ + 5 \\ \hline \checkmark 635 \end{array}$$

LONG DIVISION

Division man guides you through the steps of long division.

1. Divide

2. Multiply

3. Subract

4. Bring Down

Follow the steps: divide, multiply, subtract, and bring down. Repeat until all of the numbers in the dividend have been brought down.

Let's take a peek at each step until the division is complete.

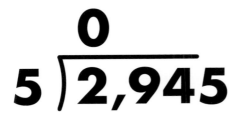

Start with the first number of the dividend. Place a 0 above the 2 in the dividend because 2 is smaller than 5.

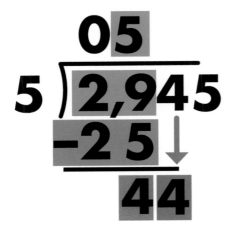

Divide: How many groups of 5 are in 29? Place a 5 above the 9 in the dividend.
Multiply 5 × 5
Subtract 25 from 29
Drop down the next digit in the dividend: 4

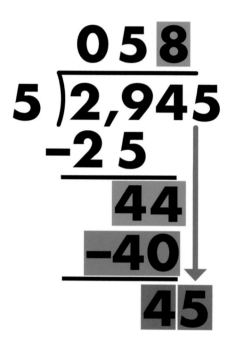

Repeat Steps:

Divide: How many groups of 5 are in 44? Place an 8 above the 4 in the dividend.

Multiply 5 ×8

Subtract 40 from 44

Drop down the next digit in the dividend: 5

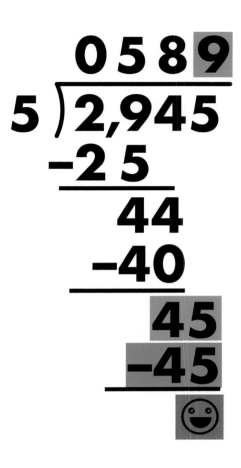

$$\begin{array}{r} 0589 \\ 5{\overline{\smash{\big)}\,2{,}945}} \\ -25 \\ \hline 44 \\ -40 \\ \hline 45 \\ -45 \\ \hline \end{array}$$

Repeat Steps:

Divide: *How many groups of 5 are in 45? Place a 9 above the 5 in the dividend.*

Multiply *5 ×9*

Subtract *45 from 45*

You are done! The remainder is zero and there is nothing left to drop down.

Check It Out!

Check your quotient:

$$\begin{array}{r} 589 \\ \times\,5 \\ \hline \checkmark\,2{,}945 \end{array}$$

Glossary

array (uh-RAY): an organized arrangement of columns and rows used to model multiplication and division

compatible numbers (kuhm-PAT-uh-buhl NUHM-burz): numbers that are easy to work with mentally

distributive property (dih-STRIB-yuh-tiv PROP-ur-tee): multiplying a group of numbers is equal to multiplying each number separately

dividend (DIV-i-dend): the number being divided up in a division problem

divisor (di-VYE-zur): the number being divided by in a division problem

equation (i-KWAY-shuhn): a math statement showing that two expressions are equal

estimate (ESS-ti-muht): a close guess used to predict a calculation

factors (FAK-turz): the number or numbers which are multiplied

inverse operations (in-VURSS op-uh-RAY-shuhnz): a math operation that reverses the result to another math operation

power of ten (POU-ur UV TEN): numbers formed by multiplying ten by itself

product (PROD-uhkt): the answer to a multiplication problem

quotient (KWOH-shuhnt): the answer to a division problem

remainder (ri-MAYN-dur): the number left over when numbers do not divide equally

Index

websites to visit

www.fun4thebrain.com/division.html

www.kidsnumbers.com/long-division.php

http://mrnussbaum.com/grade5standards/536-2/

About the Author

Lisa Arias is a math teacher who lives in Tampa, Florida with her husband and two children. Her out-of-the-box thinking and love for math guided her toward becoming an author. She enjoys playing board games and spending time with family and friends.

Meet The Author!
www.meetREMauthors.com

© 2015 Rourke Educational Media

All rights reserved. No part of this book may be reproduced or utilized in any form or by any means, electronic or mechanical including photocopying, recording, or by any information storage and retrieval system without permission in writing from the publisher.

www.rourkeeducationalmedia.com

PHOTO CREDITS: Cover: © Tammy616, CtrD, Creative_Outlet; Page 4-5: © Natallia Bokach

Edited by: Jill Sherman

Cover and Interior design by: Tara Raymo

Library of Congress PCN Data

Dive into Division: Estimation and Partial Quotients / Lisa Arias
(Got Math!)
 ISBN 978-1-62717-715-3 (hard cover)
 ISBN 978-1-62717-837-2 (soft cover)
 ISBN 978-1-62717-950-8 (e-Book)
Library of Congress Control Number: 2014935592

Printed in the United States of America, North Mankato, Minnesota

Also Available as: